MW00900463

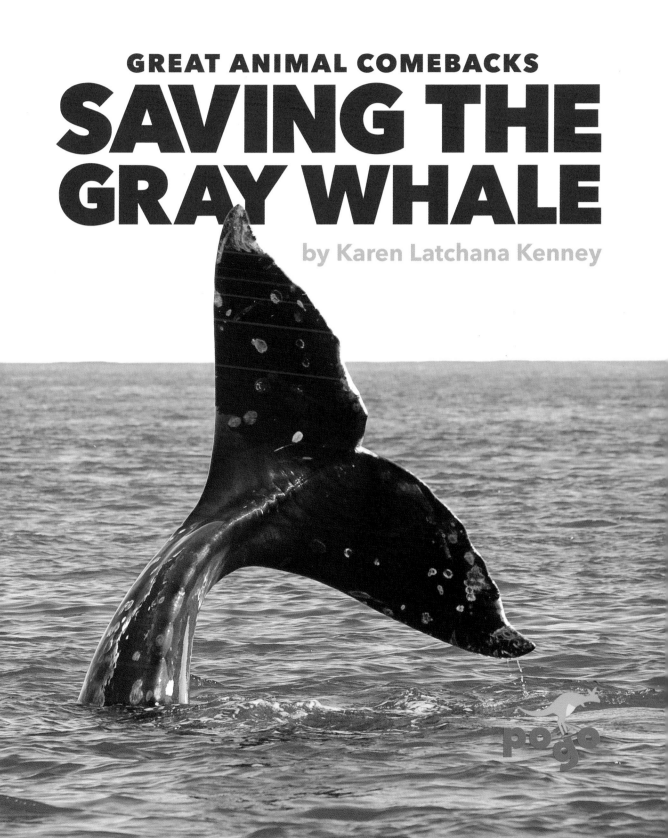

GREAT ANIMAL COMEBACKS

SAVING THE GRAY WHALE

by Karen Latchana Kenney

pogo

Ideas for Parents and Teachers

Pogo Books let children practice reading informational text while introducing them to nonfiction features such as headings, labels, sidebars, maps, and diagrams, as well as a table of contents, glossary, and index.

Carefully leveled text with a strong photo match offers early fluent readers the support they need to succeed.

Before Reading

- "Walk" through the book and point out the various nonfiction features. Ask the student what purpose each feature serves.
- Look at the glossary together. Read and discuss the words.

Read the Book

- Have the child read the book independently.
- Invite him or her to list questions that arise from reading.

After Reading

- Discuss the child's questions. Talk about how he or she might find answers to those questions.
- Prompt the child to think more. Ask: Did you know about gray whales before reading this book? What more would you like to learn about them after reading it?

Pogo Books are published by Jump!
5357 Penn Avenue South
Minneapolis, MN 55419
www.jumplibrary.com

Library of Congress Cataloging-in-Publication Data

Names: Kenney, Karen Latchana, author.
Title: Saving the gray whale / by Karen Latchana Kenney.
Description: Pogo books edition. | Minneapolis, MN : Jump!, Inc., [2019] | Series: Great animal comebacks
Audience: Age 7-10. | Includes index.
Identifiers: LCCN 2018029977 (print)
LCCN 2018031489 (ebook)
ISBN 9781641282833 (ebook)
ISBN 9781641282826 (hardcover : alk. paper)
Subjects: LCSH: Gray whale—Conservation—Juvenile literature.
Classification: LCC QL737.C425 (ebook) | LCC QL737.C425 K46 2019 (print) | DDC 599.5/22—dc23
LC record available at https://lccn.loc.gov/2018029977

Editor: Jenna Trnka
Designer: Anna Peterson

Photo Credits: Hiroya Minakuchi/Minden Pictures/SuperStock, cover, 4, 18-19; Jan-Dirk Hansen/Shutterstock, 1; MogensTrolle/iStock, 3; robertharding/Alamy, 5; Christopher Swann/Age Fotostock, 6-7; Sueddeutsche Zeitung Photo/Alamy, 8-9; The History Collection/Alamy, 10-11; Keystone/Stringer/Getty, 12; PA Images/Getty, 13; Roger Clark ARPS/Shutterstock, 14-15; Oregon State University, 16; 4FR/Getty, 17; Andrea Izzotti/Shutterstock, 20-21; Vikki Hunt/Shutterstock, 23.

Printed in the United States of America at Corporate Graphics in North Mankato, Minnesota.

TABLE OF CONTENTS

CHAPTER 1

HUNTING GRAY WHALES

Gray whales fill the San Ignacio **Lagoon**. They **breach** out of the water.

calf

Why are they here? The lagoon is off the coast of Mexico. The water is warm and calm. Gray whale mothers **migrate** here to give birth to **calves**.

baleen

They feed in these shallow waters, too. They dig their heads into the seafloor. Then they suck in mud and water. Their **baleen** catches tiny shrimplike creatures.

But this lagoon was once nearly empty. Why? These whales almost went **extinct**.

DID YOU KNOW?

Digging up mud helps other marine animals, too. How? It releases **nutrients** into the water. Other animals need these. Some animals make their homes in the crevices left behind on the seafloor.

People began hunting gray whales thousands of years ago. Native American tribes killed whales for food.

Europeans shot **harpoons** from **whaling** ships. They killed thousands of whales.

DID YOU KNOW?

There are two gray whale **populations**. The eastern North Pacific gray whales live along the western coast of North America. The western North Pacific gray whales live along the coasts of Russia, Korea, China, and Japan. Another population used to live in the Atlantic Ocean. But it went extinct in the 1700s.

harpoon

Europeans made oil from gray whale **blubber**. They used the baleen, too. In the early 1900s, large ships made whaling easier. These ships had big openings. Workers could pull whales up onto the ships. They cut them up right there. By the 1940s, only a few thousand gray whales were left.

whaling ship

TAKE A LOOK!

Europeans used baleen for many things we would now use plastic or steel for. Like what? Fishing poles. Skirt hoops. Umbrella ribs. Take a look at the gray whale's other parts.

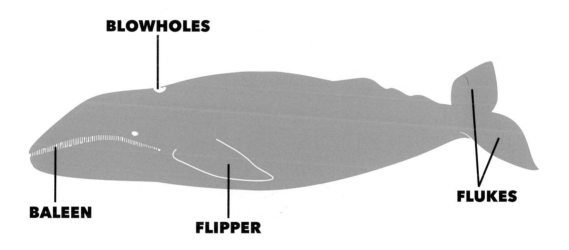

BLOWHOLES

BALEEN

FLIPPER

FLUKES

CHAPTER 2

· ·

SAVING THE SPECIES

World leaders met in 1946. They formed the International Whaling Commission (IWC). Countries agreed to stop hunting whales. How many? Only 15 at first. As of 2018, 89 countries were in the IWC.

People around the world wanted to help, too. In the 1960s, they started asking government leaders to protect this **species**.

Then in the 1970s, the Mexican government helped. They protected their lagoons. People can whale watch in some areas. But they cannot go into protected areas.

In 1973, a U.S. law helped, too. It was the **Endangered** Species Act (ESA). It protected gray whales. How? It gave states money for programs to save the whales.

DID YOU KNOW?

Some Native American tribes can still hunt gray whales. Why? They eat the whales for food. The IWC limits how many they can kill each year.

CHAPTER 3

GRAY WHALES TODAY

The western North Pacific gray whale is still on the ESA list. There are only around 200. But eastern North Pacific gray whale numbers have grown. In 1994, they were taken off the ESA list.

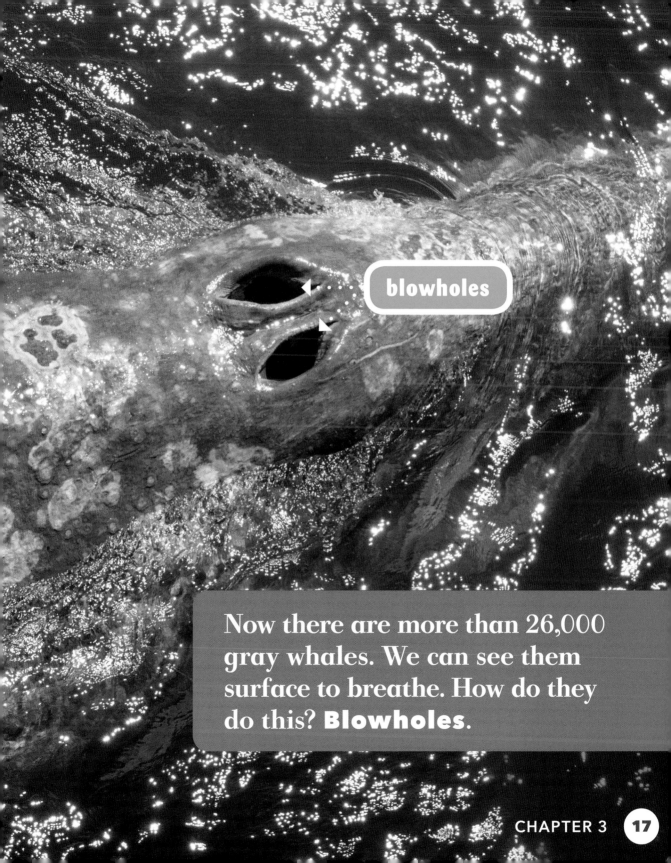

blowholes

Now there are more than 26,000 gray whales. We can see them surface to breathe. How do they do this? **Blowholes**.

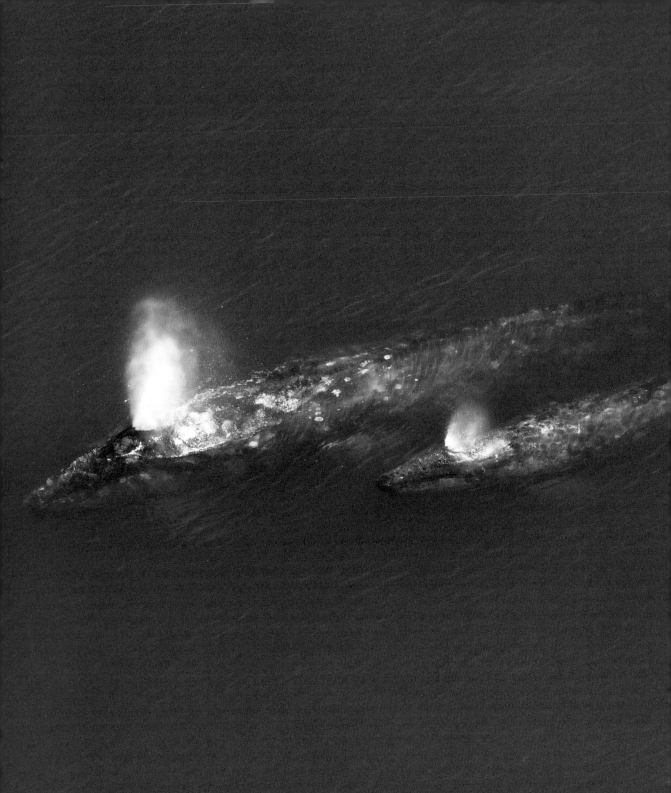

Gray whales are safer now.
But they still face dangers.
They get trapped in fishing
nets. Large ships hit them.

People can visit gray whales in lagoons. They watch them from boats. The whales are gentle. They let people touch them.

Gray whales have made a comeback. But they still need our help. What can you do to help?

ACTIVITIES & TOOLS

LISTEN TO GRAY WHALES

Gray whales make different sounds. Listen to some sounds in this activity.

What You Need:
- computer
- notebook
- pen

❶ Ask an adult to help you find gray whale sounds to listen to on a computer. Here is one site:
  • Laguna San Ignacio Ecosystem Science Program: Sounds of Gray Whales in Laguna San Ignacio:
    https://www.sanignaciograywhales.org/project/acoustics/

❷ Listen to the sounds. Take notes as you listen. What do the sounds remind you of? Do you notice patterns to their sounds?

❸ Compare them with the sounds of another kind of whale. How are they different? How are they the same?

GLOSSARY

baleen: A tough, stringy material in the mouths of certain whales, used instead of teeth for straining food from water and mud.

blowholes: Nostrils at the top of a whale's head that are used for breathing.

blubber: The layer of fat under the skin of a whale or other large marine mammal.

breach: To break through the surface of the water, as in a whale's jump out of water.

calves: Young whales.

endangered: In danger of becoming extinct.

extinct: No longer found alive.

harpoons: Long spears attached to ropes and thrown or shot from guns to hunt whales and large fish.

lagoon: A shallow body of water that is separated from the open ocean by a reef.

migrate: To move to another area or climate at a particular time of year.

nutrients: Substances people, animals, and plants need to stay strong and healthy.

populations: The total numbers of living things in certain areas.

species: One of the groups into which similar animals and plants are divided.

whaling: Having to do with the hunting, killing, and selling of whales and their products.

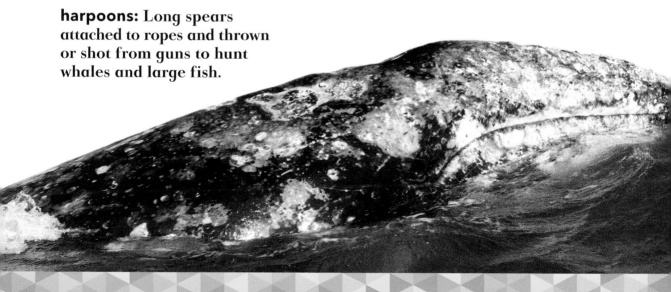

INDEX

TO LEARN MORE

Finding more information is as easy as 1, 2, 3.

❶ Go to www.factsurfer.com

❷ Enter "savingthegraywhale" into the search box.

❸ Click the "Surf" button to see a list of websites.

FACT
SURFER